H is For HISPANIC HERITAGE MONTH

Visit Our Amazon Author Page for More Books Like This

SCAN ME

Sophie DAVIDSON

Copyright © Sophie Davidson
ALL RIGHTS RESERVED

No part of this book may be reproduced, stored in a retrieval system, or transmitted in any form or by means, electronic, mechanical, photocopying, recording, scanning, or otherwise, without the publisher's prior written permission.

Hispanic Heritage Month is a time when we celebrate the history, people, and culture from Spanish-speaking countries!

#PERSONAL ALPHABET

Pick your own Alphabet about Hispanic Heritage Month

a .... n ....
b .... o ....
c .... p ....
d .... q ....
e .... r ....
f .... s ....
g .... t ....
h .... u ....
i .... v ....
j .... w ....
k .... x ....
l .... y ....
m .... z ....

A IS FOR ART

Enjoy beautiful Hispanic art.

B IS FOR BILINGUAL

Hello

Hola

Explore the beauty of being bilingual by learning Spanish words alongside English

C IS FOR CULTURE

Dive into the rich and diverse cultures of Hispanic communities, experiencing their customs and traditions.

D IS FOR DANCE

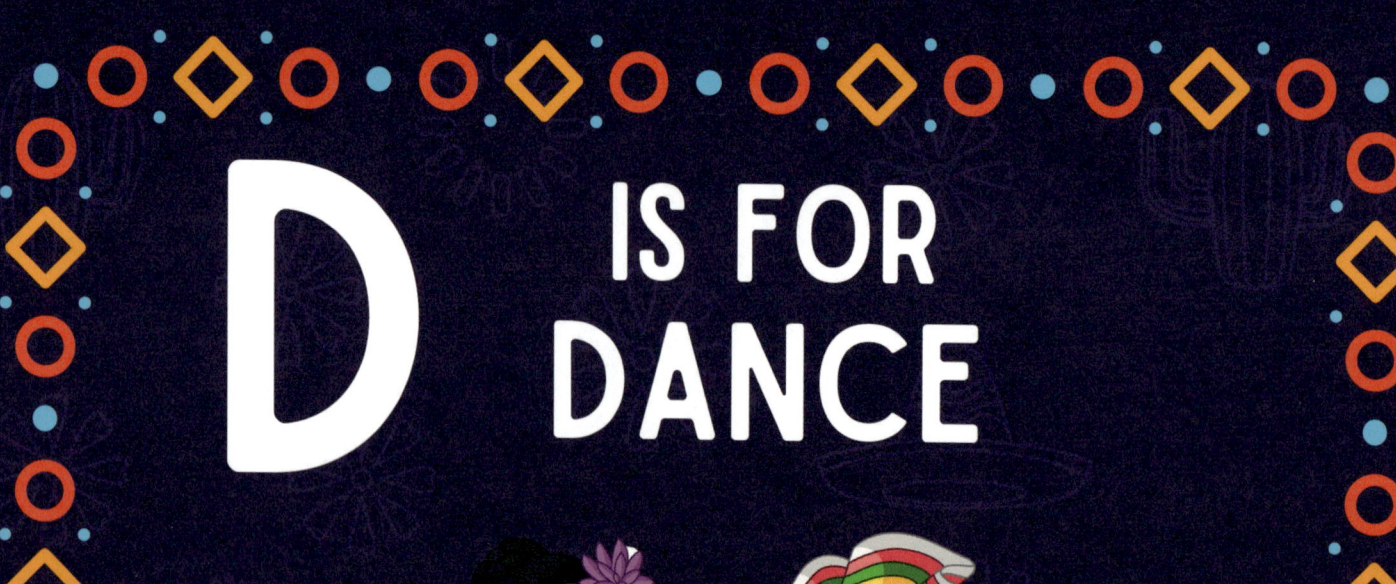

Dive into the rich and diverse cultures of Hispanic communities, experiencing their customs and traditions.

E IS FOR ESPAÑOL

The Spanish language, spoken by millions worldwide and central to Hispanic culture and communication.

F IS FOR FIESTA

Celebrate lively Hispanic fiestas, where music, dance, and vibrant decorations create a festive atmosphere.

G IS FOR GAMES

01 GALLO	02 EL DIABLO	03 LA DAMA	04 EL CATRIN	05 EL PARAGUAS
06 SIRENA	07 LA ESCALERA	08 LA BOTELLA	09 EL ÁRBOL	10 EL MELÓN
11 EL VALIENTE	12 EL GORRITO	13 LA MUERTE	14 LA PERA	15 LA BANDERA

Celebrate lively Hispanic fiestas, where music, dance, and vibrant decorations create a festive atmosphere.

H IS FOR HERITAGE

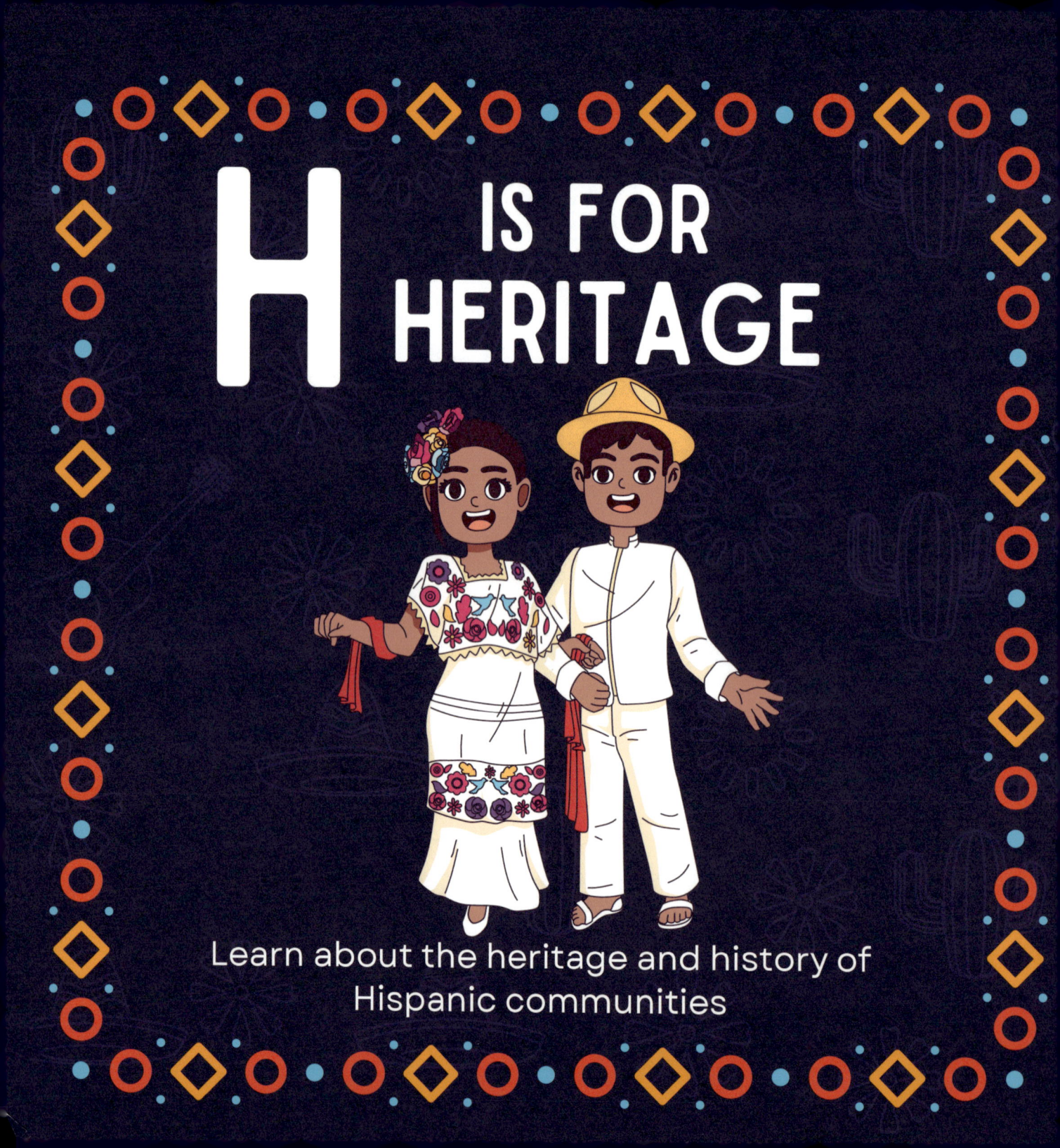

Learn about the heritage and history of Hispanic communities

I IS FOR INSTRUMENTS

Listen to the rhythmic sounds of traditional Hispanic instruments like maracas, guitars, and congas.

J IS FOR JALAPEÑOS

Jalapeños are small green peppers that add a spicy kick to many Hispanic dishes!

K IS FOR KITES

Some Hispanic countries like Guatemala and Mexico fly big, colorful kites during this month

L IS FOR LIMONADA

Hispanic countries often make limonada, a refreshing lemonade drink with a twist of lime or other fruits, perfect for hot days.

M IS FOR MUSIC

Music is very important in Hispanic cultures. There are many types of music, like salsa, merengue, and tango, that make everyone want to dance and have fun.

N IS FOR NACHOS

Nachos are crispy chips with melted cheese that are fun to eat and share during Hispanic Heritage Month

O IS FOR ORCHESTRAS

Listen to the beautiful and dynamic performances of Hispanic orchestras, showcasing classical and contemporary music.

P IS FOR PARADES

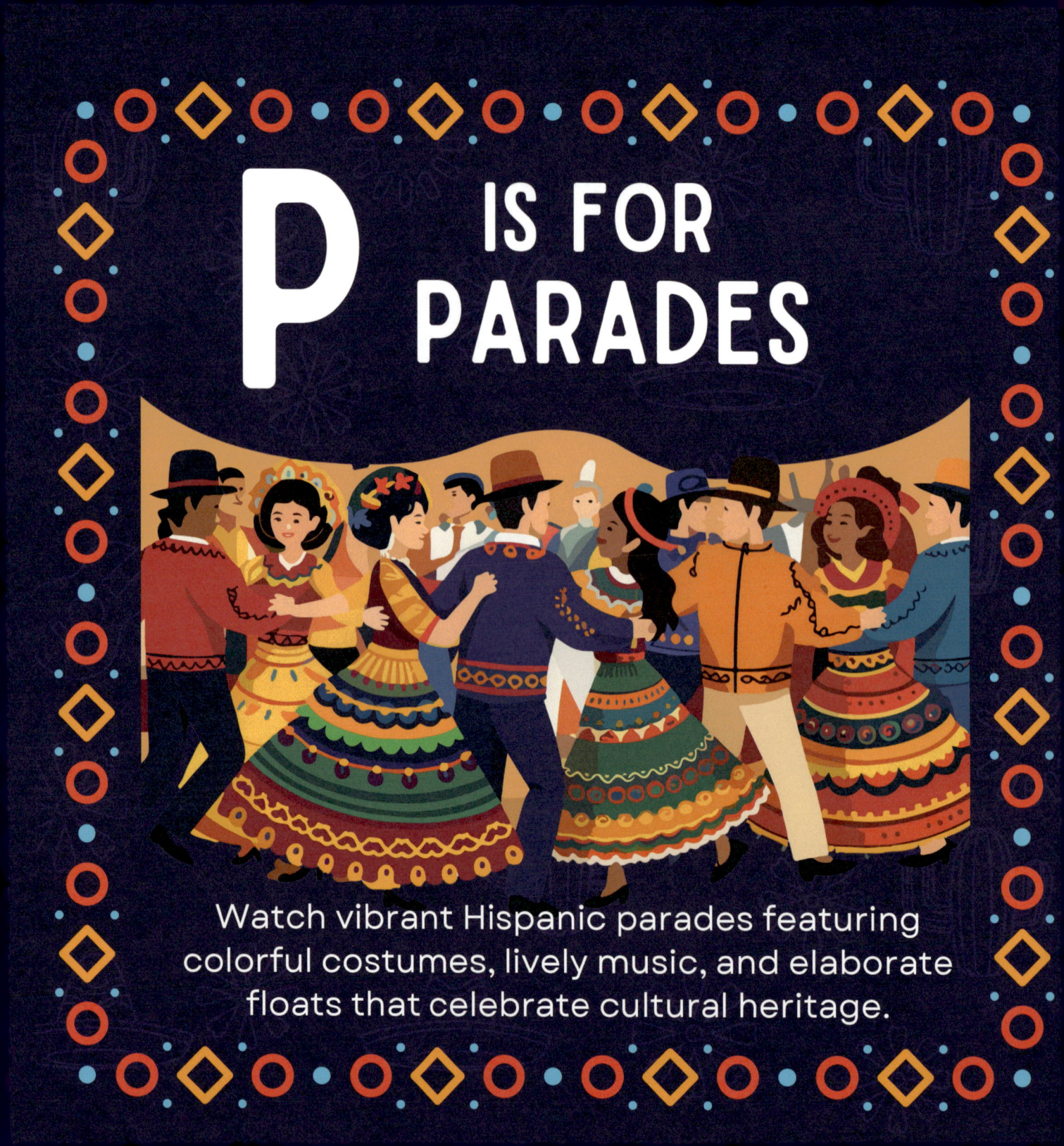

Watch vibrant Hispanic parades featuring colorful costumes, lively music, and elaborate floats that celebrate cultural heritage.

Q IS FOR QUERIDO

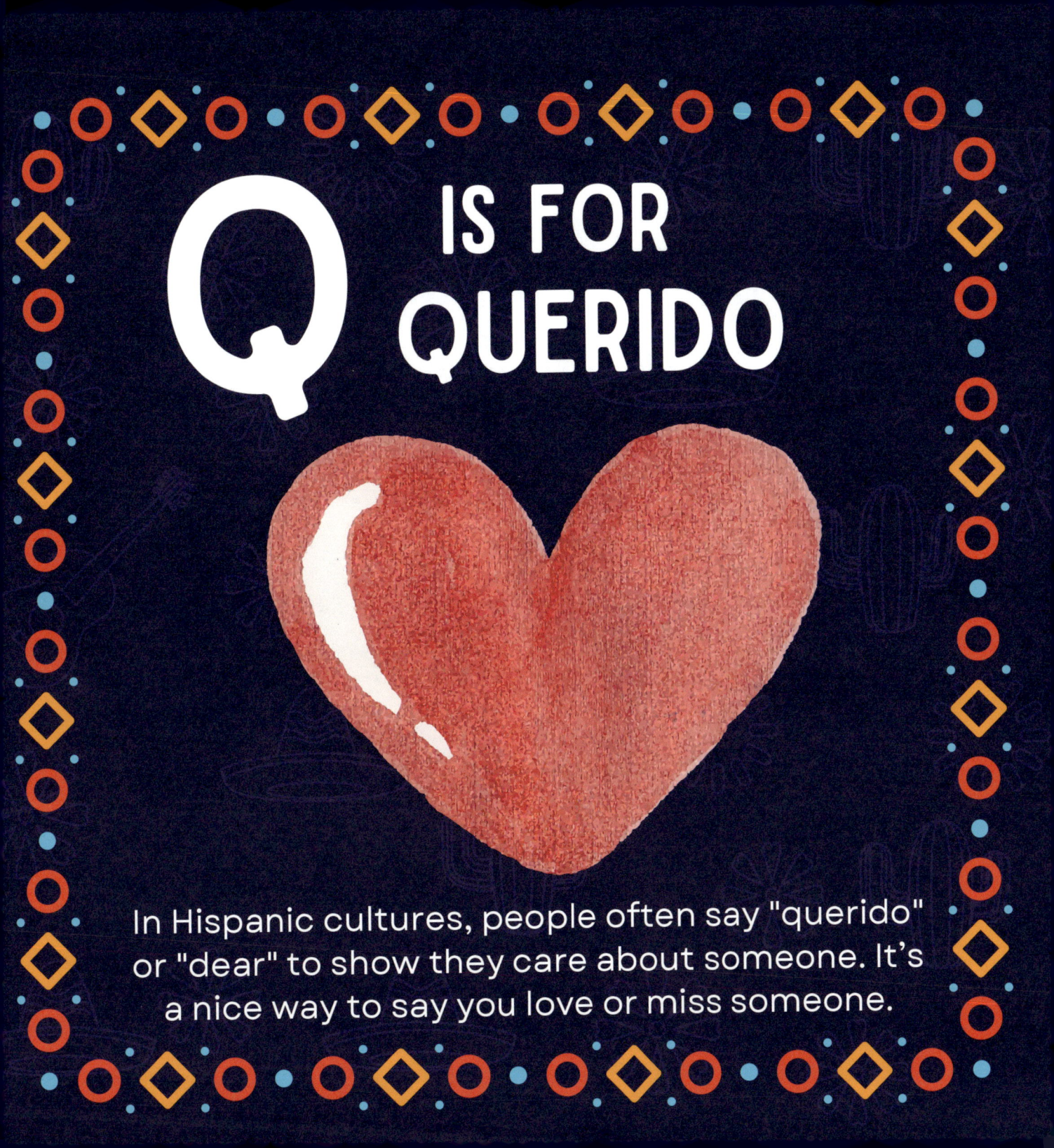

In Hispanic cultures, people often say "querido" or "dear" to show they care about someone. It's a nice way to say you love or miss someone.

R IS FOR ROPA (CLOTHING)

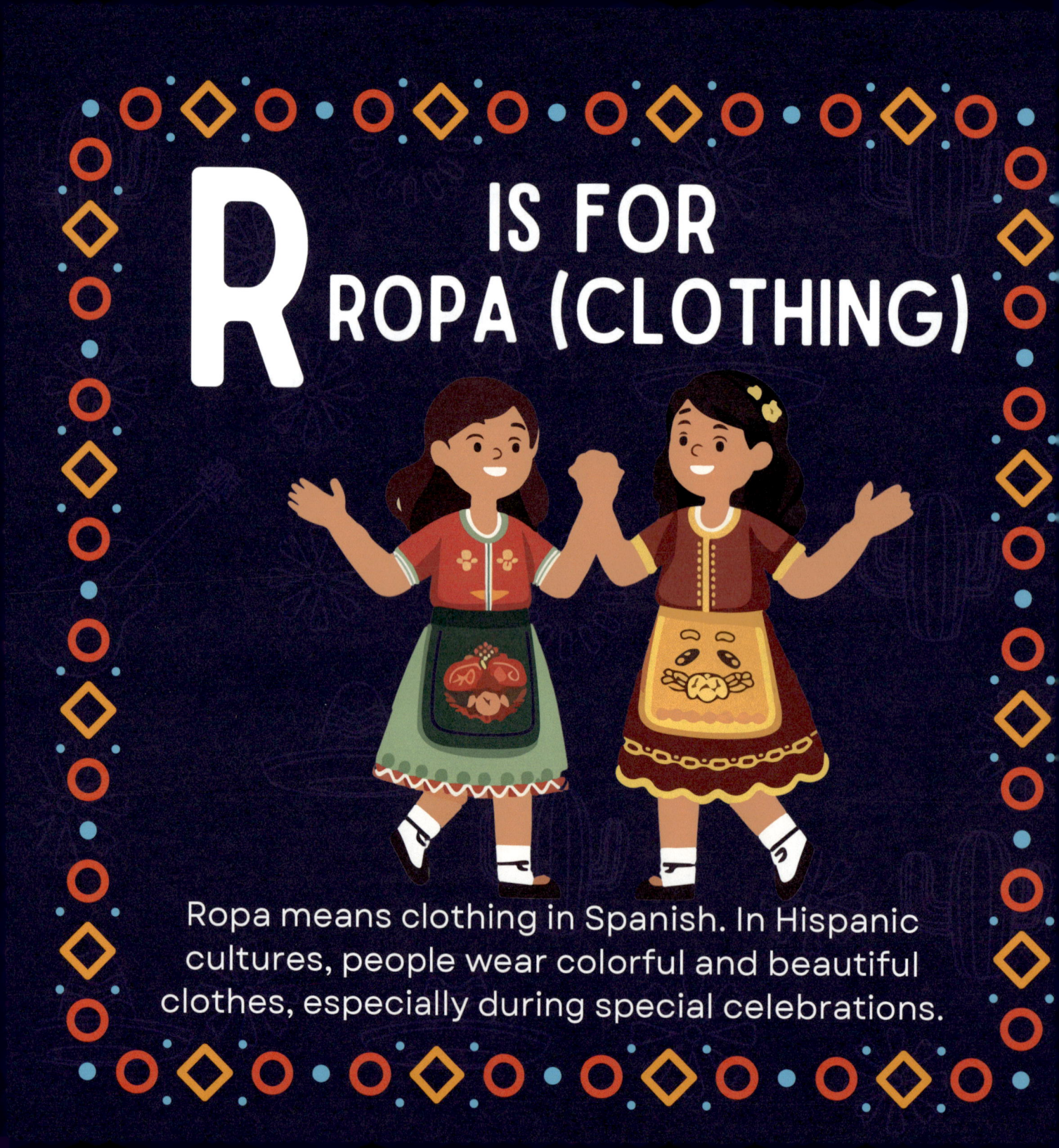

Ropa means clothing in Spanish. In Hispanic cultures, people wear colorful and beautiful clothes, especially during special celebrations.

S IS FOR SALSA DANCE

Salsa is a type of music and dance of hispanic origin.

T IS FOR TRADITIONS

Participate and learn about various Hispanic traditions, such as Dia de los Muertos.

U IS FOR UNITY

Celebrate the unity and diversity within Hispanic communities, recognizing the strength that comes from coming together.

V IS FOR VALUES

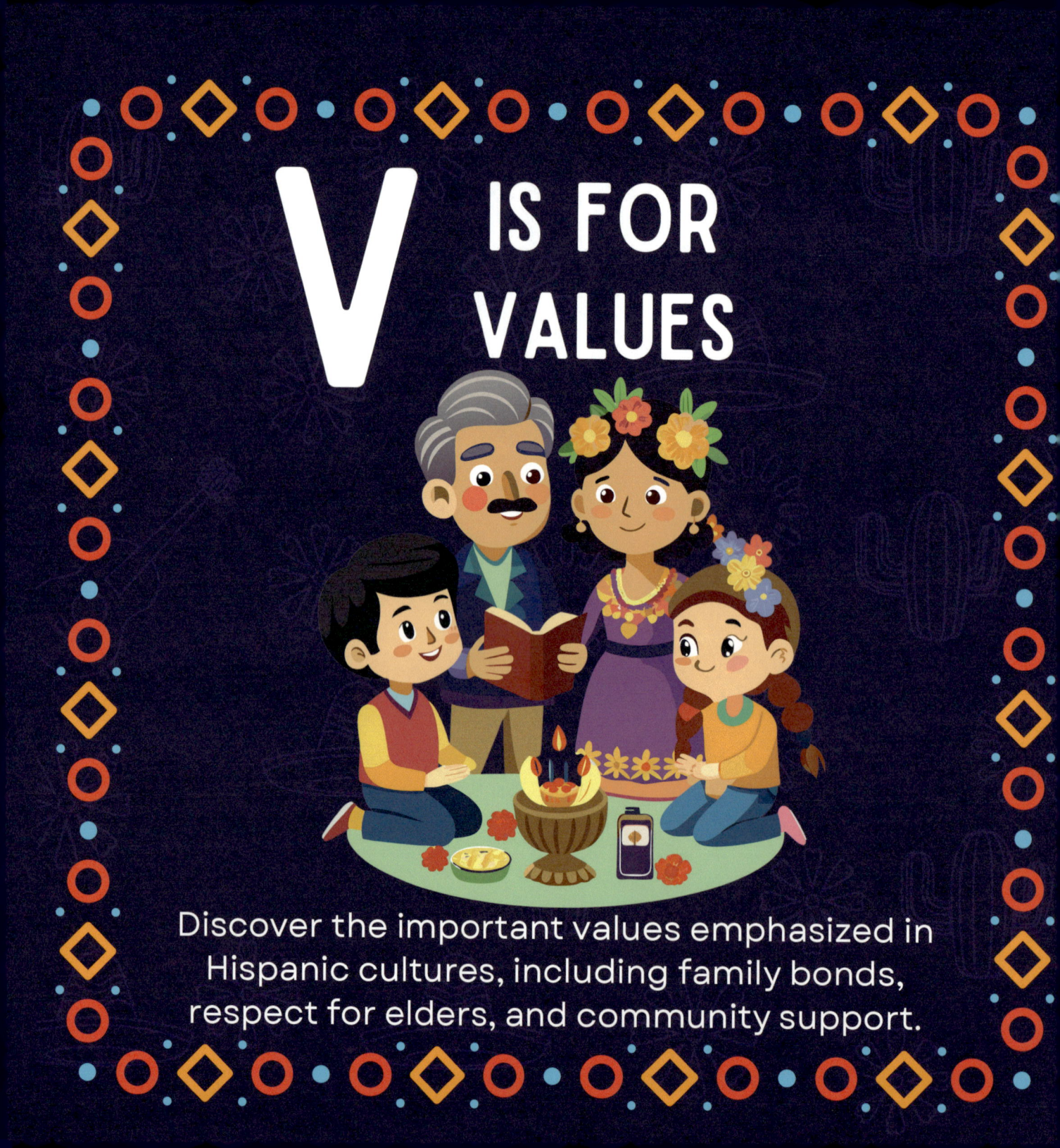

Discover the important values emphasized in Hispanic cultures, including family bonds, respect for elders, and community support.

W IS FOR WEAR

Wear traditional dress during this festival.

X IS FOR XYLOPHONE

Enjoy the sounds of the xylophone, an instrument used in some Hispanic music to create cheerful melodies.

Y IS FOR YUMMY

Taste and enjoy a range of yummy Hispanic foods, each with its own unique flavors and culinary traditions.

Z IS FOR ZUMBA

Join in on Zumba dance classes, which combine fitness and fun with energetic Hispanic-inspired music and moves.